BOOK ANALYSIS

Written by Chloé de Smet
Translated by Rebecca Neal

AF143773

Submission

BY MICHEL HOUELLEBECQ

MICHEL HOUELLEBECQ

FRENCH WRITER, POET AND ESSAYIST

- **Born in Réunion (France) in 1956**
- **Notable works:**
  - *Atomised* (1998), novel
  - *The Possibility of an Island* (2005), novel
  - *The Map and the Territory* (2010), novel

Michel Houllebecq (real name Michel Thomas) is a French intellectual and artist. His writing has made him famous across the world, and he won France's prestigious *Prix Goncourt* for his novel *The Map and the Territory* in 2010. From novels to poetry, songs to directing, and comedy to photography, he has proved himself to be a man of many talents. Widely respected in the literary world for his great talent and his works imbued with cynicism, he is also considered to be a master of polemic due to his negative comments about Islam. Houllebecq is an unusual and provocative figure and, while he may be liked by some and disliked by others, he is an integral part of the current literary landscape.

SUBMISSION

A CONTROVERSIAL NOVEL

- **Genre:** futuristic political and social novel
- **Reference edition:** Houellebecq, M. (2015) *Submission*. Trans. Stein, L. London: William Heinemann.
- **First edition:** 2015
- **Themes:** politics, religion, society, sexuality, loneliness, frustration, happiness

Published at the start of January 2015 in the wake of the *Charlie Hebdo* terrorist attacks (7 January 2015), *Submission* is a futuristic political and social novel. In a fictional version of France in 2022, François, a lonely character who leads a dull existence as a university professor, experiences drastic changes in his life when a Muslim party comes to power. In this novel, Houellebecq produces a lucid political and moral narrative in which religion is at the fore and fiction and allusions to reality intermingle. As soon as it was published, *Submission* smashed sales records in France and across Europe, and caused controversy as some accused it of fuelling Islamophobia.

SUMMARY

CHAOS AND INTERETHNIC WARS

In 2022, France is facing escalating violence between Muslim immigrants and native French citizens. Indeed, the country is on the brink of civil war following the massive influx of Muslims and the rise in extremism. Tension is high and chaos is taking over towns and cities, supported by politicians. The Indigenous Europeans Party rejects this Islamic colonisation and is preparing for a real armed struggle.

In this context François, who is a professor of literature at the Sorbonne and a specialist on Huysmans (French writer, 1848-1907), begins to worry about this very tense socio-political climate. Although his life is dreary and largely uninteresting, he pays attention to the upcoming presidential elections, which could prove to have highly improbable results. Indeed, the first round has been won by the far-right National Front party, led by Marine Le Pen (French politician, born in 1968), followed by the Socialist Party, led by Manuel Valls (French politician, born in 1962), with the Muslim Brotherhood Party a close third. Consequently, the second round will be of crucial importance. Wholly unexpectedly, the traditional social-democratic parties join forces with the Muslim party under Mohammed Ben Abbes in order to counter the Front National.

THE MUSLIM BROTHERHOOD PARTY COMES TO POWER

The results of the election are in. François sits frozen in front of his television: the Muslim Brotherhood Party has taken power. This marks the fall of social democracy, the end of the Republic and the start of the Islamisation of France. The professor wonders what consequences this change of regime will have on him, his career and his love life. All around him rumours are rife and François realises that nothing will ever be quite like it was before.

This soon proves to be the case, as the Sorbonne becomes a Muslim university and the professor is dismissed the next day. In fact, from now on only Muslims or converts can teach at an Islamic university. Of course, women are immediately cast aside. As well as forcing women to stay at home, to wear trousers or adopt the veil, the new government introduces new changes such as polygamy. As such, men can now have multiple wives (sometimes as many as six!) and sexual relations with minors are permitted.

Myriam, one of the Jewish students and François's occasional lover, is forced to leave France and return to Israel in order to follow her parents, who are terrified of the future in France. As a result, the professor, who is already solitary and pessimistic by nature, finds himself more alone than ever, jobless and aimless, with alcohol and a pension offered by the Islamic university his only comforts.

It must be pointed out that the measures imposed by the

new government, which has Mohammed Ben Abbes as its president and François Bayrou (French politician, born in 1951) as its prime minister, do pay off, as crime and unemployment rates both go down.

NEW PATH, NEW LIFE

Meanwhile, François experiences another misfortune as he learns of the death of his father, with whom he had lost contact years ago. This news, which does not particularly affect him, nonetheless forces him to return to the family home to meet his father's new partner and discuss his inheritance. He then receives a large part of his father's goods and fortune. Although he no longer has any financial worries, his loneliness and lack of activity leave him feeling completely overwhelmed. In an attempt to fill this emotional and professional void, François decides to make appointments with a series of call girls. However, he feels no pleasure with any of these different women.

In search of meaning, and above all to fight boredom, François decides to leave Paris. In order to both escape from his current life and think about his situation, he goes first of all to a small village in the Lot (France), before continuing his solitary journey to Rocamadour, which was a place of pilgrimage for Christians during the Middle Ages. Ultimately, this spiritual quest does not do him much good, so he is still looking for a purpose in life.

When he returns to Paris, he receives an offer to oversee the production of a book for the prestigious *Pléiade* series and to write a preface on Huysmans. Finally feeling wanted, and honoured to have the distinction of writing for this series, the former professor accepts this new intellectual challenge. Moreover, Robert Rédiger, the new President of Universities, offers to give him back his teaching position at the newly privatised and Islamised Sorbonne. Although he is reluctant at first, François gradually lets Rédiger convince him. Obviously, there is one condition before he can be taken on: he must convert to Islam. Seemingly convinced of the merits and expediency of this change in religion, he takes the declaration of faith known as the *Shahada*. He is all the more willing considering that polygamy and arranged marriage have certain advantages for a university professor.

Thanks to his work with the *Pléiade* and his recent conversion, François achieves a certain renown among his colleagues: he has become an acquaintance to pay attention to in the university world. Finally, he glimpses a new path and a new life that will probably be filled with wives and arranged marriages, as set out in Islam. All things considered, he has found a kind of happiness and has no regrets.

CHARACTER STUDY

FRANÇOIS

François, the narrator of the novel, is a professor at the Sorbonne and a Huysmans specialist. This fortysomething Parisian spent seven long years writing his doctoral thesis on the late 19th century French writer, whom he profoundly admires: "he had managed to write books that made me consider him a friend". As we read the book, we become aware that François and Huysmans have many things in common: loneliness, pessimism, provocation, criticism of the modern world which they see as decadent, conversion to religion, etc. As such, through this character the reader discovers Huysmans's personality and the richness of his work.

For the past several years, François has had no contact with his parents. He lives alone and has very few friends. Pessimistic by nature, he sees the end of his studies and particularly of his thesis as the end of his youth and almost his life. The future seems dull and dreary to him: "it's not as if I expected my last years to be happy. There was no reason that I should be spared from grief, illness or suffering". Because he does not want to enter the world of work, he chooses instead to become a lecturer at the Sorbonne, even though he is not at all inclined towards teaching.

From then on, he trudges through in the world of academia. His only consolation is the privileged contact he has with his female students. François is somewhat sleazy:

he enjoys sleeping with his students and spending his evenings watching pornographic videos online. Among his conquests, one young woman has particularly held his attention: Myriam. She is a literature student in love with her professor, while he gets a lot of pleasure from her. In spite of the peace of mind he feels when he spends time with her, François is not really attached to Myriam and is not prepared to make any effort to stop her from going to Israel.

Myriam sees him as a chauvinist with a paradoxical personality. On the one hand, he is erudite and sophisticated; on the other hand, he sees women as inferior and advocates a return to a patriarchal regime. Finally, he has an unclear relationship with alcohol: whether to drown his boredom or to make himself appear more attractive, François always drinks until he gives himself a bad headache.

Towards the end of the novel, he seems to have found meaning in his life thanks to his conversion and his new job as a professor in the Islamised university. Even his sexual and relationship problems seem to disappear, since Islam permits arranged marriages and polygamy. In any case, François is a solitary, detached, borderline obscene man, and as readers we hesitate to feel either revulsion or pity for this character.

MYRIAM

Myriam is a 22-year-old modern literature student. She comes from a Jewish family and is intelligent and sure of herself. She is François's last conquest before his conversion to Islam, and he describes her as "a very classy young woman, with her bobbed black hair, her white skin and her dark eyes. Classy, but quietly sexy". Their relationship has been going on for several months, but remains unstable because of their regular break-ups. Myriam feels more than just physical attraction towards her professor and falls in love with him, but does not explain this to him. Indeed, she hates a number of aspects of François's personality, in particular his chauvinist and disillusioned side. Her exile, caused by the social and political tensions in France, makes her give up on this paradoxical love. A few months later she builds a new life in Israel and tells François via email.

MARIE-FRANÇOISE TANNEUR

Marie-Françoise is a brilliant colleague of François's and works at the Sorbonne. She is a specialist on Balzac (French writer, 1799-1850) and is always the most well-informed person on the regulations and new measures linked to the university. When the new government comes to power, the fact that she is a woman means that Marie-Françoise must end her career and stay at home. With few natural attractions and physically ungraceful, Marie-Françoise is nonetheless pleasant and likeable. François appreciates her qualities and the valuable information she provides about the university: "I liked the old bag. She was funny, she was an insatiable gossip, and she'd been at the university long enough, and spent enough time on the right committees, to have better information than anyone would ever entrust to the likes of Steve".

ROBERT RÉDIGER

When the Muslim Brotherhood Party comes to power, Robert Rédiger is appointed President of Universities. The former professor is a talented and ambitious man. He greatly admires François, whom he considers a distinguished intellectual because of his brilliant thesis on Huysmans. In the last part of the novel, Robert makes his colleague an offer to return to his teaching post at the newly Islamised university. In order to convince him, he uses his talents as a speaker and flatters him on every front, to the point where François has no choice but to accept his proposition. While keeping his position as director, Robert is also appointed Secretary of State for Universities, a post which was created during the cabinet reshuffle.

ANALYSIS

A FUTURISTIC POLITICAL NOVEL

Submission can be described as a futuristic novel, because it imagines our world in a more or less distant future. In this case, the author immerses us in a "post-Hollande" (French politician, born in 1954) France, during a turbulent election season and at a time of unprecedented chaos. Another characteristic of the futuristic novel is that it is believable. It is therefore a matter of anchoring the narrative in the real world so that readers can envision themselves there. Reading the text, we quickly understand that Houellebecq uses this approach by mixing fiction – Islam seizing power – and allusions to reality – mentions of French public figures such as François Hollande, Marine Le Pen, François Bayrou, David Pujadas, Jean-François Copé, Lionel Jospin, etc. Indeed, in present-day France, which is increasingly marked by immigration and political setbacks (resignation of the government, unemployment, instability, the rise of the National Front, the failure of centrist parties, etc.), there is almost nothing fictional about the story Houellebecq tells us.

This novel can also be considered as a satire on current French politics, as well as a scathing analysis of our modern way of life. In fact, at a time when France is undergoing a genuine socio-political crisis, *Submission* appears as a mocking and clear-sighted critique of the country. Through his subtle use of irony, the author highlights the blindness, and even the narrow-mindedness, of some leaders. Whether through implicit allusions – "For a moment I thought his inner man of the left had been roused, then I reasoned with myself: his inner man of the left was fast asleep, and nothing less than a political shift in the leadership of the French university system could ever rouse him" – or explicit attacks – "The foreign press looked on, bewildered, as a leftist president was reelected in a country that was more and more openly right wing: the spectacle was shameful but mathematically inevitable" – François Hollande and his policies are heavily criticised. The far-right party led by Marine Le Pen is also mocked and criticised. Indeed, here the National Front is depicted as an identity-based movement marked by "the embarrassing antisemitism of its leader". Finally, our current way of life and the vacuity of our society of hyperconsumerism are also subject to the author's sarcastic comments. Houllebecq's irony can be found particularly in his cutting descriptions of a contemporary world which basks in a kind of playful comfort.

> "Microwave dinners were reliably bland, but their colourful, happy packaging represented real progress [...] There was no malice in them, and one's sense of participating in a collective experience, disappointing but egalitarian, smoothed the way to a partial acceptance."

Furthermore, the author also attacks Western liberalism through a lucid and clinical analysis. As such, in his view this individualistic and materialistic political doctrine has destroyed traditional society. France's founding principles (work, education, family, religion, etc.) are thus called into question, and the Republic as we currently know it seems to have lost its reason for existing.

In addition to the political aspect, in this work Houellebecq deals with the religion of Islam and its extremes by imagining the unprecedented situation of Islam taking power: polygamy, arranged marriages, the subordination of women, the end of atheism, single-sex schooling, the supremacy of Muslims, etc. Following Ben Abbes's electoral victory, upheaval and even anarchy are expected. However, it must be pointed out that the new government's gamble has paid off. By soothing tensions and bringing order back to society, the Islamic religion appears to have saved and benefitted the people. For Rédiger, Islam is called upon to dominate the world in both political and religious terms. He also sees other beliefs, such as Christianity or Buddhism, as inferior: "He quoted Nietzsche's AntiChrist: 'If Islam despises Christianity, it has a thousandfold right to do so; Islam at least assumes that it is dealing with men…'"

In this way, at once very close to and too far from present-day France, Houellebecq presents us with a work that is twisted and disconcerting, because it casts doubt on our beliefs and certainties. It is also a deeply troubling futuristic novel, because it brilliantly depicts the process at work in the collective unconscious.

A DESPERATE SEARCH FOR HAPPINESS

> "'It's submission,' Rédiger murmured. 'The shocking and simple idea, which had never been so forcefully expressed, that the summit of human happiness resides in the most absolute submission.'"

This line, spoken by Robert Rédiger in the novel, can shed light on the meaning of the novel's title. The title "submission" can thus be understood as the submission of man before God in the Islamic religion, but also as the submission of women to men. To go further, it can even evoke the submission of an entire society before the government. According to the President of Universities, in Islam, man's capacity to submit to God is an undeniable source of fulfilment. Consequently, through these words Houellebecq leads us to reflect on earthly happiness and on the close ties between man and his religion.

At the end of the work, François agrees to convert to Islam and to thus change his way of life. How can this conversion be understood? Opportunism or a desperate attempt? Taking into account François's personality, a case can be made for both of the two motives. Closely linked to despair, the concept of "dereliction" can also be used to explain this change in religion. This feeling of abandonment and moral solitude (definition from the *Larousse* dictionary) is in fact characteristic of François's temperament. Alone and deprived of affection for too long, he has created a world for himself where he is the only protagonist. In search of spiritual fulfilment, he has turned first of all to Huysmans, then to monasteries and other places of worship. Unfortunately, these last journeys fail to provide the answers he is so desperately seeking. His pursuit of happiness seems futile until Rédiger lets him back into the university. As such, while remaining an unbeliever, the professor seems to have found a kind of happiness in his "submission" to Islam.

HOUELLEBECQ'S CYNICISM

Houellebecq, who is known for his cynical and acerbic writing, gives us in this book a perfect demonstration of his style. With a bold disregard for propriety and public opinion, in *Submission* he draws a simplistic and caricatural portrait of Islam (men have the option of polygamy, while women are forced to wear the burka). He is therefore not afraid to shock by playing with caricatures and he does not hesitate to express ideas which go against all social and moral codes. For example, he evokes a shocking parallel between the Nazi movement in the 1930s and the rise of Islam in the West: "History is full of such blindness: we see it among the intellectuals, politicians and journalists of the 1930s, all for whom were convinced that Hitler would 'come to see reason'".

This offbeat and provocative side has earned him his share of problems and enemies. Indeed, *Submission* was immediately seen by some politicians and elements of the media as a racist work which encourages the xenophobia of the National Front. Consequently, for the launch of his book Houellebecq gave an increased number of interviews and media appearances in order to explain the ins and outs of his book. In spite of all his efforts to calm tensions, impassioned criticisms arose and the work was pirated a fortnight before its release. In addition, in the face of the tragic terrorist attacks on the newspaper *Charlie Hebdo*, the writer decided to cancel the promotional tour for his book. In this context of fear and violence, Houellebecq even received death threats and has since been living under permanent police protection.

FURTHER REFLECTION

SOME QUESTIONS TO THINK ABOUT...

- The narrative opens by praising literature. In your opinion, what is the meaning of this passage?
- The book includes the line "If Islam is not political, it is nothing". According to Rédiger, Islam is called upon to dominate the world. What is your opinion on this matter?
- The novel imagines the end of atheism and humanism. In the current context, in what way can *Submission* be considered a futuristic novel?
- Rédiger says "That Europe, which was the summit of human civilisation, committed suicide in a matter of decades." What link(s) can you think of between the themes of this novel and the future of Europe?
- To what extent can the character of François be considered an antihero? Develop your argument using examples from the book.
- In your opinion, is François responsible for his desperate situation? Apart from conversion, what other option(s) might he have had?
- Since its publication, *Submission* has been accused of fuelling Islamophobia. What is your opinion on this matter?
- In the novel, Houellebecq closely links sexuality and religion. In your opinion, what was his aim in choosing this approach?
- In your opinion, is an Islamised France possible and imaginable one day?
- Throughout the novel, François brings up Joris-Karl

Huysmans. How would you justify the omnipresence of this writer?

We want to hear from you!
Leave a comment on your online library
and share your favourite books on social media!

FURTHER READING

REFERENCE EDITION

- Houellebecq, M. (2015) *Submission*. Trans. Stein, L. London: William Heinemann.

REFERENCE STUDIES

- Website of Michel Houllebecq http://www.houellebecq.info

MORE FROM BRIGHTSUMMARIES.COM

- Reading guide – *The Map and the Territory* by Michel Houellebecq

Les Amours Sauvages

Grégory Menchon

Édition : BoD-Books on Demand,
12-14 rond-point des Champs-Élysées, 75008 Paris
Impression : Books on Demand, Norderstedt, Allemagne

ISBN : 978-2-3222-1044-2
Dépôt légal : Mai 2020

J'exulte encore quand tes plaisirs
Vagabonds, sonnent à ma porte,
De nonchalant je deviens vif,
Tant tu me plais et me transportes.

Et tant qu'un simple jeu s'installe,
Où le flou borde nos brefs échanges,
On fait taire les voix incessantes,
De nos cicatrices qui dérangent.

Donc à cœur joie, dans le paraître,
Sans que le raisonnable nous freine,
On se dévore à perdre la tête,
On oublie les casseroles qu'on traine.

Ça dure un temps, ça dure longtemps,
Mais jamais plus cette promesse,
Celle d'être plus que des amants,
C'est quand on s'aime que l'on se blesse.

J'voulais nous faire extraordinaires,
Des fous d'amour sans une tâche,
Des doux rêveurs, des visionnaires,
Je souhaitais juste que tu le saches.

J'aurais mis ma vie aux enchères,
Pour enfin partager la tienne,
Mais me lancer, j'aurais dû l'faire,
Avant que ta vie soit la sienne.

Et de cocu je deviens roi,
Abject, que le bonheur effleure,
Amour défunt d'un cœur de bois,
Qui n'a que faire de tes pleurs.

Affranchi de tes lèvres assassines,
Et vide de candides regrets,
J'inhibe sans mal l'image coquine,
De ton corps nu et singulier.

Et si tes mots me touchent encore,
Amour poison né de chimères,
Je serais froid comme la mort,
À contre cœur pour te déplaire.

Et je traverserais l'amère,
Envie de te savoir loin,
Sur des bateaux, vieux comme la Terre,
Où les ivresses me tendent la main.

Je devins aigre et indolent,
Imparfait inconnu qu'on ne saurait taire,
Criant justice et justement,
Cet inconnu me mit à terre.

Comme un songe qu'on ne croirait pas,
Extatique, je ne l'attendais plus,
Et je folâtre et même parfois,
Je me supporte sans avoir bu.

Tu n'es qu'une âpre parenthèse,
Qu'il a su vite en moi souiller,
Et comme une bruine qui m'apaise,
Il est si beau, il est si vrai.

Dès lors défiant toute certitude,
Sombre jaloux tu reviendras,
Nouvelles promesses, nouveau prélude,
Pour ne m'avoir rien que pour toi.

Mais je tuerai tes envies folles,
De me dompter à nouveau,
Car ton cœur est trop frivole,
Et m'a battu la fois de trop.

Et je briserai tes vains espoirs,
Boirai tes larmes jusqu'à plus soif,
Pour qu'à ton tour à ton départ,
Tu vois ton cœur en épitaphe.

En lune, lové dans tes courbes,
Je goûte à tes formes et tes sueurs,
Et aux caprices de tes doigts fourbes,
Bien entiché de ton odeur.

Je pardonne tes coquins affronts,
Quand tu cherches à me résister,
Car ça n'est jamais bien trop long,
Et tu r'viens toujours implorer.

Je brave encore des interdits,
Invente de banales mises en scène,
Pour faire le tour de ta literie,
Mais rester séducteur bohème.

J'arrête les vaniteux prologues,
Plus b'soin d'paraître à tes côtés,
J'mets sur pause l'amour catalogue,
Avec toi, j'arrête de jouer.

Des heures à perdre, qu'est-ce qu'on en a,
Quand plus rien d'autre autour ne compte,
Et qu'on s'habille juste de tes draps,
Pendant que nos ardeurs s'affrontent.

Osons enfin prendre la route,
Prenons les armes, que l'on s'affaire,
À cribler de balles tous nos doutes,
Et fendre enfin, nos cœurs de pierre.

8

Je change d'armure pour être plus fort,
Troque mes armes contre des histoires,
Sans lendemain et sans remords,
Un peu fleur bleue, un peu bâtard.

J'vendrai du rêve en bon menteur,
Et m'amuserai de ces louanges,
Qu'il fût un temps touchaient mon cœur,
Je s'rai démon dans un corps d'ange.

Je n'resterai plus dans le flou,
Des interrogations profondes,
Mes mots ne vaudront plus un clou,
Un chant d'violon sans qu'on m'accorde.

Je resterai aventurier,
Palpant des cœurs sans démesure,
Corps contre corps pour m'amuser,
Sans que l'on sente mes impostures.

Et vous n'y verrez que du feu,
Mais pas celui qui s'est éteint,
Jusqu'à c'que je perde à mon jeu,
Et qu'je veuille plus lâcher ta main.

Allez, mets-moi une claque,
Que ça fasse mal pour que j'te hais,
Que ça m'dégoute, que j'fasse des lacs,
Immenses de larmes pour t'oublier.

J'ai plus la force de continuer,
À te fixer allègrement,
De jouer un rôle et d'espérer,
Que tu m'regardes tendrement.

Que ton message soit enfin clair,
Que tes silences soient déchiffrés,
Il y a bien pire que d'te déplaire,
Comme prétendre vouloir t'ignorer.

Mets-moi une claque quand j'te dirai,
Que j'veux ta bouche pour m'apaiser,
Que j'veux tes bras pour m'enlacer,
Et que rien d'autre pourrait compter.

Dis-moi qu'des films on s'en fait tous,
Et qu'on dérape comme on respire,
Et qu'on déraille la peur aux trousses,
En ignorant toujours le pire.

J'peux pas rester dans cet état,
Je me déteste quand j'me déguise,
Que ça fasse mal mais juste une fois,
Donne-moi l'envie de lâcher prise.

Que m'as-tu fait, je suis en vrac,
Un palpitant qui m'enivre,
Je manque de cran, je manque de tact,
Mes pensées sont à la dérive.

Tu te pointes en fier insoumis,
Cachant tes douleurs et tes peines,
Bouscules mes jours, perturbes mes nuits,
Me fais esclave sans qu'on m'enchaîne.

Ton innocence a fait mouche,
Je suis conquis, deviens chasseur,
Tu te dévoiles, couche après couche,
Je veux ta bouche, je veux tes sueurs.

Tu fais de moi un seau de larmes,
Que je déverse à l'occasion,
Lorsque tes yeux dans ce vacarme,
Me font perdre la raison.

Tu es l'irrésistible poison,
Qu'il serait vain de ne pas goûter,
Je veux te boire, ma déraison,
M'a pris au piège, je suis poings liés.

Ce verre de plus se boit sans mal,
Le mal est fait de toute façon,
J'ai mal de t'être juste banal,
J'ai mal tu sais d'être aussi con.

Tu me parasites dans mes vers,
Tu vois, j'écris quand ça s'arrose,
Les soirs de mou où pour te plaire,
J'étale mes rimes, je jette ma prose.

J'sais pas quoi faire car t'es partout,
Te détester ? même pas en rêve,
J'ai mal de toi j'suis comme un fou,
Mais je mets mes pleurs en grève.

Un verre de trop, toi tu t'en fous,
Je bois mes verres comme tes paroles,
Car tu me mènes jusqu'au dégoût,
De mon âme et d'ses envies folles.

T'es pas commun, j'ai l'mal de toi,
Mais ton indifférence me tue,
À petit feu mais tu sais quoi ?
En vrai c'est fou, j'suis d'jà foutu.

T'es pas l'premier qui m'aura pris,
Mon amour propre en bon salaud,
Mais j'garde espoir et j'garde envie,
Même si t'es pas l'bon numéro.

Dans ses bras je t'ai vu nu,
Et j'en ai perdu la raison,
Mais cette première déconvenue,
Ne fut pas ma dernière leçon.

Car de néfastes habitudes,
Se sont installées dans ton lit,
Avec l'insolente certitude,
De pouvoir masquer tes folies.

Il serait vain pour toi de croire,
Que tes téméraires escapades,
Restent sous ton unique bon vouloir,
Et que j'ignore cette mascarade.

Achevé, je te laisse faire,
Je suis éploré mais complice,
Je ne s'rai pas l'amour austère,
Qui entravera tes caprices.

Je serais prêt à tout subir,
Même tes idylles vagabondes,
Et j'exulte de tous les voir fuir,
Lorsque tes tromperies abondent.

Tu es une folie enivrante,
Qui me tue et qui m'inspire,
Ma passion véhémente,
Pour le meilleur et pour le pire.

J'ai repris mon pied dans l'alcool,
À puer l'ivresse d'un nous bateau,
J'préfère encore puer la gnole,
Y'à pas qu'à toi que j'suis accro.

Amer de quoi, de ton manège ?
Où sur ton socle tournent des cœurs,
Qui se rêvent tous uniques, mais piège,
T'es comme ce vin, j'ai mal au cœur.

En passent encore des beaux minois,
Qui chaque jour te tournent la tête,
J'n'échappe guère à tes règles à toi,
J'ai pas l'roman mais juste l'en-tête.

Ce fameux soir tu m'as surpris,
À n'pas repousser mes avances,
J'voulais hurler le cœur conquis,
Que j't'aimais plus que tu n'le penses.

Quand ta froideur m'a pris de court,
J'savais qu'ma place était d'jà prise,
Alors j'lève mon verre sans discours,
À mes échecs, à ta bêtise.

À notre éphémère rencontre,
Et à toi qui auras su taire,
La simple envie de me corrompre,
Et d'resourire, juste pour te plaire.

Je t'ai vu lui prendre la main,
Nul besoin de vous cacher,
Vous étiez là, comme des gamins,
Pas vus pas pris, ça tu connais.

J'ai déposé sur la commode,
Un bout de papier griffonné,
Je sais qu'ça n'est plus à la mode,
Mais les crises de larmes c'est surfait.

J'ai rangé mes rêves au placard,
Vidé mon sac la fois de trop,
Pris quelques chemises au hasard,
Là où tu caches tous ses cadeaux.

Et puis j'ai pris le premier train,
Le premier verre, le premier venu,
Noyé mon futur, mon chagrin,
Dans cet hôtel qui t'avait plu.

Je n'attendrai plus que tu viennes,
La bouche en cœur plein de promesses,
J't'ai plus dans la peau, dans les veines,
Mais je pardonne tes maladresses.

Mes appels vains, comme des échos,
Ont fait leur route mais s'évaporent,
Tu n'es plus rien, un vice de trop,
Une ancienne blessure indolore.

Enfin j'arrive à reconnaître,
Ton vicieux manège et tes lois,
Fallait du temps je dois l'admettre,
Mais tu n'abuseras plus de moi.

Je fus ton sauveur autrefois,
Lorsque naïfs on s'inventait,
Alors loin de tes doux tracas,
Une vie de bohèmes torturés.

Que l'on me pende pour trahison,
Si de toi je rêve encore,
Je ne goûterai plus au poison,
De tes mots, ton rire, ton corps.

Je n'serai plus la bonne épaule,
Lorsque tes aventures s'épuisent,
Et que mon cœur corniaud s'affole,
Lorsque tu reviens, sans surprise.

Tu n'seras plus l'enfant terrible,
Que j'adulais encore hier,
Et bien que ça me soit pénible,
J'me ferai démon, juste pour te taire.

Je n'écrirai plus une lettre,
Pour raisonner ton âme folle,
Qu'il fût un temps je pensais prête,
À renier ces frissons frivoles.

Je mettrai mes souvenirs en gage,
Et je m'offrirai le silence,
Que j'étalerai quand de passage,
Tu reviendras tenter ta chance.

C'est bon j'arrête, je coupe les ponts,
Tu me traiteras, d'homme puéril,
De marginal ou de démon,
Mais j'pars avant qu'le temps défile.

J'ai pt 'être la force d'un agneau,
Et le courage d'un gamin frêle,
Mais quand je fuis, quand tout est trop,
Je nous évite bien des querelles.

Ne m'en veux pas, t'as tout à perdre,
Dans cette histoire que l'on s'invente,
Je vois déjà les belles emmerdes,
Ton mépris et mes vaines attentes.

Tu l'vois même pas, j'suis pas pour toi,
J'ai soif d'amour et de passion,
Mais quand vient l'aube d'un toi et moi,
J'ai peur de nous, de mes démons.

Tu me diras que j'ai eu tort,
Et que la vie est faite de risques,
Me donneras, bien des remords,
Mais j'y crois plus, changeons de disque.

Il a tes jambes, sans être tendre,
Fourrure d'hiver, toison salée,
Avec un goût à s'y méprendre,
Et je me laisse encore valser.

Et il m'opère sans une mi-temps,
De tous ses doigts peu délicats,
La belle affaire, un coup dans l'vent,
Parce qu'il semblait un peu comme toi.

Il a tes mains, grandes et joueuses,
Mais lui ses claques me font bien mal,
Il a aussi des lèvres pulpeuses,
Mais d'une tendresse animale.

Parce qu'il a, tout comme toi,
Un caractère un peu sanguin,
Ce soir j'ai la marque de ses doigts,
Sur mes joues vierges de tes mains.

Mais parce qu'il est un peu de nous,
À l'heure où toi tu n'es plus là,
Je m'en contente, j'accuse le coup,
Parce qu'il semble un peu comme toi.

Ô quel petit oiseau volage,
Suspect, je t'ai pris au nid,
Dans son grand lit, sa grande cage,
Et je n'étais même pas surpris.

J'aurais souhaité que d'un présage,
Je puisse deviner l'issue,
Ta bêtise me dévisage,
Et ton indifférence me tue.

Alors en fuite avec mes vices,
Je bâtirai, à m'en rendre marteau,
Une tour d'ivoire et de délices,
Où je m'égare en bon salaud.

Aveugle et sourd je me donnerai,
À l'hypocrite démesure,
Et quand vient l'aube je disparais,
Comme on enlève une salissure.

Et tu pourras te reprocher,
Que notre histoire n'était qu'un leurre,
Quand viendra le temps de pleurer,
Rigide et froid mon joli cœur.

Je t'ai laissé me surprendre,
Dans ce grand bar peu fréquenté,
Un dédaigneux cœur à prendre,
Que tu vas sans doute malmener.

Regard fuyant mais je te suis.
Je suis, hagard mais démasqué,
Et malgré nos claires envies,
Tu me dévoiles tes noirs secrets.

Baiser volé me met à terre,
Entre deux verres, entrelacés,
J'te laisse m'atteindre, c'est de bonne guerre,
Je tombe le masque, désarmé.

Tu aimes, mes rouages défaillants,
Et mes caprices effrontés,
Mes regards coupables et prudents,
Mes désirs anxieux et cachés.

Tu es d'une implacable adresse,
Dans ce vacarme et sons cortège,
De vils actes, de maladresses,
Et je veux être, seul dans ton piège.

Alors je frôle le ridicule,
Mais ne serai plus un martyr,
Plus de points, que des virgules,
Et toute une vie pour te l'écrire.

À tort ou à raison, je te hais,
Toi qui as bouleversé mon âme,
Comment peut-on autant aimer,
Un si petit bout de femme ?

Que des échos dans chaque rue,
Des débris d'espoirs effrontés,
Vestiges de câlins assidus,
Et de rêves qu'on a partagé.

Je suis le courage qu'on enchaîne,
Transi de honte de ne pouvoir,
Surmonter la peur et la haine,
De ton immanquable départ.

Mon désespoir, mon vague à l'âme,
Face à la mer le cœur voilé,
Me rendent fou, dans ce vacarme,
Je veux les taire et me noyer.

Et je persiste à te revoir,
À perdre pied je continue,
Mais tu n'es plus quand je m'égare,
Celle pour qui mon cœur a battu.

Je paye, indûment notre histoire,
Hurlant sur ton corps étendu,
Contre ce silence chaque soir,
Contre ce cancer qui te tue.

Des nuits entières à te chercher,
Rêveuse quand tu te perds,
Entre mes hanches dans tes pensées,
Je manque d'amour mais tu manques d'air.

Je veux connaître tes faiblesses,
Sous ton opaque manteau,
De larmes puis de chaudes allégresses,
Et de discours à demi-mots.

Mais quand je flirte avec l'ivresse,
Pour te rejoindre dans la folie,
Je te l'accorde je manque d'adresse,
Pour mettre à nu ton cœur meurtri.

Vois-tu ma candide rébellion,
Face à ton revêche caractère ?
Tu me blesses plus que de raison,
Sans que je mérite ta colère.

Je dois creuser sous tes barrages,
Tant ce salaud lui t'a brisée,
Tu as mis mon amour en cage,
Et je suis pieds et poings liés.

Tu sais on n'est pas tous les mêmes,
Même si tu connais la chanson,
Viens sur le devant de la scène,
Avec moi, chasse tes vieux démons.

Je veux que tu goûtes au plaisir,
D'une journée sans larmes versées,
Et que tu me laisses te séduire,
Sans plus devoir te supplier.

J'ai vu bien assez de terres sales,
Pour savoir maintenant que c'est toi,
Je n'veux plus être un coup banal,
Mais bien celui que tu aimeras.

Alors sois rebelle à ta guise,
Mais sois-en sûre je reste là,
Tu es de loin la plus exquise,
Des insoumises mais moi j'y crois.

J'ai maintenant pris pour habitude,
De te cacher mes intentions,
Pour que s'installe un jeu absurde,
De dissimulée séduction.

J'aime effleurer ta peau curieuse,
Loin d'être amère à ce manège,
Te donner des envies furieuses,
Sans que tu te sentes pris au piège.

J'aime te regarder perdre pieds,
Quand je m'amuse en un regard,
À te convoiter sans bouger,
Et perturber ce grand gaillard.

Il faudra te faire une raison,
Perdre la mienne n'est plus à faire,
Tu n'obtiendras de toute façon,
De moi rien d'autre, c'est de bonne guerre.

Dans mes ballades je suis en laisse,
Je perds le contrôle de mes mains,
Tu peins mes rimes et maladresses,
Tu guides mes mots, j'me sens crétin.

Mais ce matin je deviens barge,
J'pars tout lâcher au bord de l'eau,
Car comme toi j'voudrais prendre le large,
Mais il faut qu'on m'remette à flot.

Sur la jetée les vagues dégueulent,
Branches et déchets à la dérive,
Y'a pas qu'la mer qui se sent seule,
Y'a ce grand con qui reste ivre.

Où sont parties nos folles idées,
Quand sur le perron avec toi,
Nous préparions tant de virées,
En s'embrassant bien trop de fois ?

Où sont passées tes vagabondes
Mains, aussi belles que cochonnes,
Avant ces déconvenues immondes,
Qui ont fait de moi cet ivrogne ?

Où a donc sombrée notre histoire,
Dans tes grands océans de larmes ?
C'est quand même pas la mer à boire,
Que d'enfin déposer les armes.

T'es le seul à jouer d'la gâchette,
Et même tes mots sont assassins,
Mais cette fois pas même une lettre,
Cette fois j'ai pas vu v'nir la fin.